Horses and Ponies

Cathy Beylon

Dover Publications, Inc.
Mineola, New York

Bibliographical Note

Let's Color Together—Horses and Ponies, first published by Dover Publications,
Inc., in 2013, contains all the plates from *Horses and Ponies,* originally published
by Dover in 2006.

International Standard Book Number

ISBN-13: 978-0-486-77974-4
ISBN-10: 0-486-77974-2

Manufactured in the United States by RR Donnelley
77974205   2016
www.doverpublications.com

Note

Horses and ponies at play, on the farm, and at work, are waiting for you to bring them to life with color. Ponies love to have fun, and here you will see them taking a stroll with a furry friend, trying to catch a butterfly, and even taking a swim. On the farm are horses getting new shoes, having a snack, and relaxing in the field. Busy at work are ponies giving rides and posing for pictures at the ranch, and horses performing tricks at the circus. There are also scenes from the pony show, and a portrait of the first place winner!

In this special coloring book, part of the *Let's Color Together* series, each page is printed twice, so you can share this exciting coloring adventure with whomever you choose—a friend, sibling, or a parent are just some ideas. The easy-to-remove, perforated pages make it simple to share coloring pages. Try coloring pictures at the same time, and then have fun comparing your color choices!

Bunnies love ponies, too!

Bunnies love ponies, too!

What a beautiful day to go for a walk!

4

What a beautiful day to go for a walk!

It's time to relax with a friend.

It's time to relax with a friend.

Mother keeps a close watch on her pony.

Mother keeps a close watch on her pony.

Horses love to graze on grass.

Horses love to graze on grass.

Ponies are so playful!

Ponies are so playful!

Ponies don't stray far from their mother.

Ponies don't stray far from their mother.

These ponies are best friends.

These ponies are best friends.

Let's go for a swim!

Let's go for a swim!

It's time for a drink.

It's time for a drink.

Good morning!

Good morning!

It's feeding time.

It's feeding time.

Horseshoes help protect the horse's hooves.

Horseshoes help protect the horse's hooves.

Horseback riding is so much fun.

Horseback riding is so much fun.

The Nature Trail is beautiful!

The Nature Trail is beautiful!

Horses enjoy being groomed.

Horses enjoy being groomed.

This is my favorite pony.

This is my favorite pony.

It's time for a bath.

It's time for a bath.

Let's go for a ride.

Let's go for a ride.

The ponies at the ranch are so friendly.

The ponies at the ranch are so friendly.

It's fun to visit the Pony Ranch.

It's fun to visit the Pony Ranch.

You never forget your first pony ride.

You never forget your first pony ride.

I look just like a cowboy.

I look just like a cowboy.

Hayrides are a lot of fun!

Hayrides are a lot of fun!

Stay on the path so you don't get lost.

Stay on the path so you don't get lost.

Let's go jumping.

Let's go jumping.

We came in first place!

We came in first place!

The prize pony.

The prize pony.

Horses perform tricks at the circus.

Horses perform tricks at the circus.

This is my favorite circus act.

This is my favorite circus act.